THE TRIUMPH OF LOVE

BY
MARIVAUX

TRANSLATED BY
JAMES MAGRUDER

DRAMATISTS
PLAY SERVICE
INC.

for Irene Lewis

THE TRIUMPH OF LOVE was presented by Center Stage (Irene Lewis, Artistic Director; Peter W. Culman, Managing Director), in Baltimore, Maryland, in October, 1993. It was directed by Irene Lewis; the set design was by Neil Patel; the costume design was by Jess Goldstein; the lighting design was by Mimi Jordan Sherin; the composition and sound design were by John Gromada and the stage managers were Keri Muir and Julie Thompson. The cast was as follows:

LÉONIDE, A PRINCESS DISGUISED
   AS PHOCION .... Pamela Gray
CORINE, LÉONIDE'S MAID-SERVANT,
   DISGUISED AS HERMIDAS .... Kristine Nielsen
HARLEQUIN, VALET TO HERMOCRATE ..... Jefferson Mays
DIMAS, GARDENER TO HERMOCRATE .... Jarlath Conroy
AGIS, A PRINCE, RAISED BY HERMOCRATE ...... Jay Goede
LÉONTINE, SISTER TO HERMOCRATE .... Judith Marx
HERMOCRATE, A PHILOSOPHER............. Mario Arrambide

THE TRIUMPH OF LOVE was presented by Classic Stage Company (David Esbjornson, Artistic Director; Patricia Taylor, Managing Director), in New York City, on March 29, 1994. It was directed by Michael Mayer; the set design was by David Gallo; the costume design was by Michael Krass; the lighting design was by Brian MacDevitt; the original music was by Jill Jaffe; and the production stage manager was Crystal Huntington. The cast was as follows:

LÉONIDE, A PRINCESS DISGUISED
   AS PHOCION .... Margaret Welsh
CORINE, LÉONIDE'S MAID-SERVANT,
   DISGUISED AS HERMIDAS .... Camryn Manheim
HARLEQUIN, VALET TO HERMOCRATE ..... Daniel Jenkins
DIMAS, GARDENER TO HERMOCRATE .... Ümit Çelebi
AGIS, A PRINCE, RAISED BY
   HERMOCRATE .... Garret Dillahunt
LÉONTINE, SISTER TO HERMOCRATE .... Randy Danson
HERMOCRATE, A PHILOSOPHER........... Thom Christopher
CELLIST .... Christine Gummere

CAST

LÉONIDE, under the alias of PHOCION
CORINE, under the alias of HERMIDAS
HARLEQUIN
DIMAS
AGIS
LÉONTINE
HERMOCRATE

SETTING

The gardens of the philosopher Hermocrate in ancient Greece.

TRANSLATOR'S NOTE

I have assisted at the births of three wildly different productions of THE TRIUMPH OF LOVE, and, at the risk of sounding like a killjoy or a control freak, I would like to offer the following observations about the text in rehearsals and production.

a) Language is a friend. In Marivaux, language is something to be savored and deployed like a weapon, a character in its own right.

b) The shifts in tone and diction and the double entendres in the translation are completely intentional.

c) Respect that confusing backstory. If discovered, the Princess could be killed for what Cléomenes and Léonides did to each other.

d) Contrary to expectations, the audience will **not** throw things at Phocion for being so heartless and manipulative. They love her deceptions, especially if they believe she adores Agis.

e) Phocion: You adore Agis and would do anything to win his love, even if he does seem slow at times.

f) Agis: You are not slow; you are an innocent who is a fast learner.

g) Hermocrate and Léontine are real obstacles, not buffoons.

h) Phocion: Hide your transitions and stay on the offensive. You **love** yourself in this.

i) Love is delightful and love is cruel, leaving victors and victims in its wake. Marivaux honors both extremes in his wonderful play.

—James Magruder

THE TRIUMPH OF LOVE

ACT ONE

Phocion and Hermidas enter.

PHOCION.   Here we are — the gardens of Hermocrate the philosopher. I think.

HERMIDAS.   But Madame, we don't know anyone here. We'll be thought rude for entering so boldly.

PHOCION.   No, the gates were open, and we've simply come to speak to the master of the house. *(Pause.)* At last I have time to explain all you need to know.

HERMIDAS.   Well, that makes me breathe easier. But Princess, grant me a favor: permit me to question you as *my* fancy suits.

PHOCION.   As you wish.

HERMIDAS.   You quit your court, you leave the city. You bid me to follow. We arrive at your country estate without a retinue.

PHOCION.   That is correct.

HERMIDAS.   You know I have learned to paint — for my own amusement. We are hardly in the country for a week when you produce two portraits and ask me to make copies of them in miniature. One, a man of fifty and the other, a woman of ... let's round her off at forty-five. Both attractive enough.

PHOCION.   If the truth be known, then —

HERMIDAS.   No, I'm asking the questions. As soon as I finish copying the portraits, you suddenly announce that you're indisposed — you absolutely cannot be seen. Then you dress me up as a man, gussy yourself up in the same way and we leave incognito in your coach-and-four! Now you're calling yourself Phocion, and I am Hermidas — I might have

7

picked my own name at least. After fifteen minutes on the road, we ditch the coach and here we are in the garden of Hermocrate, a man whose philosophy I don't think you've got much reason to get mixed up with.

PHOCION.   More than you imagine, Corine.

HERMIDAS.   So why the fake illness? And the copied portraits — who are the man and the woman? What about these outfits? What about Hermocrate's garden? What do you want with him? What do you want with me? Where are we going? What will become of us? Whence leads this? Tell me quick or I'll die!

PHOCION.   Are you finished? Listen to me and please pay attention. *(Pause.)* As you know I happen to rule over these lands by accident. I occupy the throne that my uncle Léonides, the great general, usurped from the King, Cléomenes. What you don't know is that once, when my uncle was away commanding his sovereign's troops, Cléomenes fell in love with Léonides' wife, my aunt. He abducted her. Léonides, in rage and pain, attacked Cléomenes with his own armies and imprisoned the guilty pair.

HERMIDAS.   *(Interrupting.)* What about my needs?

PHOCION.   After several years he died —

HERMIDAS.   Who?

PHOCION.   The King, Cléomenes. In prison. His wife —

HERMIDAS.   Your aunt —

PHOCION.   Right — died six months later, in childbirth, bequeathing a prince to this world. This heir was kept hidden from Léonides. My uncle died in turn, heirless, mourned by his people, who saw fit to have my father rule. I myself have acceded to this tainted throne.

HERMIDAS.   Wonderful. But what the hell does this have to do with our breeches or the portraits? That's what I want to know.

PHOCION.   Watch your mouth. This prince, who first drew breath in a prison cell, who was kidnapped at birth by an unknown hand, this prince unknown to my father and uncle, I have news of this prince!

HERMIDAS. May the heavens be praised. He's under your rule.

PHOCION. No, Corine. It is I who shall place myself under his.

HERMIDAS. You my lady, you'll do nothing of the kind! I will never endure this — I swear it! *(Pause.)* What do you mean?

PHOCION. If you would but hear me out. For twelve years this prince has been in the care of the wise Hermocrate. Euphrosine, a relative of Cléomenes —

HERMIDAS. Who's Euphrosine?

PHOCION. Does it matter at this point? Don't interrupt me! Euphrosine, a relative of Cléomenes, sent him to Hermocrate to raise seven or eight years after he disappeared and ...

HERMIDAS. And? AND?

PHOCION. And ... that's all I know. I learned this from a servant who once worked for Hermocrate and his sister.

HERMIDAS. A servant! Listen, you'd better certify the tale before you go off half-cocked like this —

PHOCION. Certification is not what I am after. *(Pause.)* I wanted first to see Agis. Yes, Corine, that is his name. Agis. I found out that he and Hermocrate take walks every day in the forest near my château. So I left the city and came straight here to see him. That wily servant led me to a young man reading in thick vegetation. *(Pause.)* Until that moment I had often heard people speak of Love. It was only a word to me. Imagine, Corine, imagine a collection, an assemblage of all that we find noble and attractive in the Graces — imagine that and you will scarcely have begun to imagine all the charms to be found in the form and features of Agis.

HERMIDAS. What I'm beginning to imagine is that this charm bracelet is what's dragged us into the bush.

PHOCION. As I withdrew, Hermocrate appeared and stopped to ask me whether the Princess took strolls in that forest. He didn't know who I was. I told him, my heart pounding, that it was said she did walk in those parts. Then I rushed home.

HERMIDAS. A strange encounter indeed.

PHOCION. Stranger still has been my behavior since I saw Agis. I feigned illness so we could travel here. My name is Phocion so when I meet Hermocrate, I can beg his permission to stay awhile and profit from his wisdom. I'll talk to Agis and try to sway his heart to my ends. He cannot discover my true identity, for I was born of a blood he must revile. Before I can reveal myself, Love will have to shelter my charms from his wrath. I know he hates me.

HERMIDAS. If you say so. But my lady, what if, under this three-piece suit Hermocrate recognizes a certain young lady he met trespassing in the woods? You won't get within ten feet of the house.

PHOCION. I've thought of that, Corine. *(Darkly.)* Should he recognize me, so much the worse for him. I've set a snare that all his science can't keep him from falling into. I hope he won't force me to use it, but Love and Justice are my inspiration. I only need two or three meetings with Agis, and I'll do anything to obtain them — even debunk one measly philosopher.

HERMIDAS. What about the sister? From the looks of her portrait, a prude like that won't submit to the presence of a handsome stranger like yourself.

PHOCION. So much the worse for her too. If she blocks my path, I'll treat her no better than her brother.

HERMIDAS. Trick them both ... hmmmm. And resorting to deceit — twice over — doesn't offend you?

PHOCION. *(An outburst.)* It disgusts me! Yet my motives are praiseworthy and my mission is blameless. I must avenge myself upon Hermocrate and his sister. Since Agis has been in their care, they've taught him to loathe me! Without knowing me, without sounding the depths of my soul, filled to the brim as it is with Heaven's virtues, they paint my features in vile and hideous tints! Corine, they have mustered an army of enemies for me to battle. Even now they're raising fresh troops! *(Hermidas gives her a look.)* I do not merit their calumny. Is it because I occupy a throne usurped? Look not to me as usurper, I say — the legitimate heir has yet to come forth — he's been kept hidden in this very garden. Oh, how they wrong me! Corine, I shall act without scruples! *(Pause.)* Now hang onto those portraits you made and don't ask questions. For the time being, just do as I do and don't act surprised. When you need to know more, I'll keep you abreast. *(Harlequin enters unseen.)*

HARLEQUIN. Who are those two?

HERMIDAS. This is a mighty piece of work, my lady — our sex —

HARLEQUIN. *(Surprising them.)* Aha! "My lady" "Our sex" Out with it, my good men, you're women!

PHOCION. Heavens above! Unmanned so quickly! *(They attempt to escape.)*

HARLEQUIN. No no no — my sweet things, before you run off, we have to arrive at an understanding. I took you first for two scamps; oh how I mistook you. You are two scampi.

PHOCION. We're lost, Corine.

HERMIDAS. Let me handle this, my lady. Fear nothing. This man's face doesn't fool me — he looks quite manageable.

HARLEQUIN. I'm a man of honor, beyond all price. I'll admit I've never smuggled your sort of contraband through customs, but the merchandise stops here. I'll have the gates shut tight.

HERMIDAS. Well, don't let *me* stop you. You shall be the first to repent of the wrong you do us.

HARLEQUIN. Show me some repentance, and maybe I'll let you pass. *(Phocion gives him several pieces of gold.)*

PHOCION. Proof for starters, my friend. Now wouldn't you have been sorry to have lost that?

HARLEQUIN. You have a point, since I'm so happy to find it.

HERMIDAS. Still feel like making a scene?

HARLEQUIN. I'm only just beginning to feel like not making one.

PHOCION. *(Giving him some more coins.)* Repent further.

HARLEQUIN. Funny, my bad mood has been cut short all

of a sudden. Well then, my ladies, have you anything to declare?

HERMIDAS.   A bagatelle. My mistress saw Agis in the forest. One look and she couldn't help but rend her heart to him.

PHOCION.   *Render.*

HERMIDAS.   Same difference.

HARLEQUIN.   Touching.

HERMIDAS.   My mistress, who is rich, independent, and eligible, would like to make him sensitive to her feelings.

HARLEQUIN.   Very touching.

HERMIDAS.   As far as we know, the only way to tenderize him is to engage him in conversation and sleep in his — *(Phocion coughs delicately.)* — house.

HARLEQUIN.   You mean share in all his comforts?

HERMIDAS.   I like that you're bright. Now my lady can't do that walking around here in her own sex, am I right? Hermocrate wouldn't allow it. Agis himself would flee, given his philosophic rearing.

HARLEQUIN.   And how. Love in this house? The combined wisdom of Agis, Hermocrate, and Lady Léontine creates the most learned obstacle Love could ever dare to meet. *(Pause.)* Mine is the only wisdom with any breeding in it.

PHOCION.   We could tell.

HERMIDAS.   So you see why my lady has chosen this disguise? So you see how there's no harm done?

HARLEQUIN.   I can think of nothing more reasonable. My lady fell in love, by the by, with Agis. What of it? Let each take what he can, say I. There are plenty of hearts to go around. Have courage, gracious mistress ... I mean, person. I offer you my services. You have lost your heart — do your best to catch another's. I'd give mine up, if I could only find it.

PHOCION.   Count on my pledge, sir, and you shall enjoy a fate all men might envy.

HERMIDAS.   And don't forget — she's Phocion, and I'm Hermidas.

PHOCION.   Above all, Agis is never to know who we are.

HARLEQUIN.   Fear nothing, Lord Phocion — *en garde,* Comrade Hermidas — you see my gift for swordplay?
HERMIDAS.   Shhhh ... someone's coming. *(Dimas, the gardener, enters.)*
DIMAS.   Who's that you're talking to, friend?
HARLEQUIN.   Two personages.
DIMAS.   Hell, I can see that, but who are they? What do they want?
PHOCION.   I wish to see Lord Hermocrate.
DIMAS.   This ain't the way to go about it; master said no one's allowed tromping through the flower beds, so just turn yourselves around, go on out the way you come in, and knock at the front gate.
PHOCION.   I found the garden gate open; are strangers not permitted to make mistakes?
DIMAS.   I don't give permission for any such of a thing. I never heard tell people could come in where they please — waltz through the gates — should have the decency to call the gardener, and beg his privilege — be nice to *him.*
HARLEQUIN.   You are speaking to a rich and important person.
DIMAS.   I can see he's rich. Me, I'm the gardener — he can go 'round front. *(Agis enters.)*
AGIS.   Dimas, what are you railing about?
DIMAS.   Youth, sir. These tree-tromping youths.
PHOCION.   You have arrived, sir, in time to disencumber me. My only wish is to speak to Lord Hermocrate. I found the garden open. I found the gardener rude.
AGIS.   Dimas, please notify Léontine that a visitor worthy of esteem, even yours, wishes to speak to Hermocrate. *(Dimas exits.)* I ask your complete pardon, good sir, for this rustic welcome. Hermocrate will also wish to make his excuses to someone whose physiognomy and bearing command respect.
HARLEQUIN.   They're a *pair* of pretty faces.
PHOCION.   If I have been handled brusquely, your courtesies repair everything. And if my physiognomy, whereof you speak, inclines you to wish me well, then my features have never given better service.

AGIS.   Although it has only been a moment since we met, I assure you that one could not be more favorably inclined toward someone than I am for you.

HARLEQUIN.   Looks to me like we'll have four pretty inclinations between us.

HERMIDAS.   Why don't we take a walk and discuss ours? *(Hermidas and Harlequin exit.)*

AGIS.   Sir, may I ask for whom I declare friendship?

PHOCION.   Someone who willingly swears eternal friendship in return.

AGIS.   I fear making a friend whom I might soon lose.

PHOCION.   Sir, if it were up to me, we would never lose one another. *(Pause.)*

AGIS.   What do you want with Hermocrate?

PHOCION.   His reputation brought me here. I was seeking his permission to spend some time in his company. Now, after meeting you, my motive is far more pressing. I wish to gaze at you as long as it is possibly ... possible.

AGIS.   And then what?

PHOCION.   And then I don't know. That will be in your hands. I shall consult only you.

AGIS.   Then I advise you not to lose sight of me.

PHOCION.   Then we shall always remain together.

AGIS.   I wish it with all my heart.

HARLEQUIN.   *(Entering with Hermidas.)* My mistress is advancing, and it looks like she's got her heavy carriage on today. *(Léontine and Dimas enter.)*

DIMAS.   Look milady, there's the strange squire. That other one is his train.

LÉONTINE.   I have been informed, sir, that you ask to speak to my brother. He is not here at present. Might you confide in me?

PHOCION.   I have a favor to ask, Madame, one you yourself could grant.

LÉONTINE.   Explain yourself, sir.

PHOCION.   My name is Phocion, Madame. The name is perhaps known to you. My father, whom I lost several years ago, placed it in some repute.

LÉONTINE.   Proceed.

PHOCION.   Alone and independent am I, traveling to school my heart, instruct my wit —

DIMAS.   And shake the fruit off the trees.

LÉONTINE.   You may go, Dimas. *(Dimas exits.)*

PHOCION.   My travels take me to men whose knowledge and virtue distinguish them from all others of my sex. Some of these illustrious gentlemen have allowed me to live awhile with them. I was hoping that wise Hermocrate would not refuse me this honor.

LÉONTINE.   To look at you, sir, you seem worthy of such virtuous hospitality — from others. It is impossible for Hermocrate to extend such an honor. Important reasons — you know them, Agis — prevent it. Allow me to reveal them to you.

HARLEQUIN.   Hold on. I can keep one of them in my room.

AGIS.   We don't lack for rooms.

LÉONTINE.   No. But you know better than anyone why it cannot be permitted, Agis. We've made it our law never to share our retreat with anyone.

AGIS.   Surely it would not violate our law to make an exception for a friend of virtue.

LÉONTINE.   I cannot alter the law.

HARLEQUIN.   *(Aside.)* Tough as old boots!

PHOCION.   Madame, I see that you are inflexible to my laudable intentions.

LÉONTINE.   Yes, despite myself.

AGIS.   Hermocrate shall amend this legislation.

LÉONTINE.   I remain firm. As I am certain of his firmness.

PHOCION.   *(Aside to Hermidas.)* I shift to Plan B. *(Aloud.)* Madame, I withdraw my suit. But might I ask for a private audience with you?

LÉONTINE.   Further entreaties are useless, sir; you shall only annoy me. However, if you insist upon it, I consent.

PHOCION.   I do insist. Please withdraw for a moment. *(Agis exits. Aside.)* May Love see fit to smile upon my stratagem. *(Aloud.)* Since you are unable, Madame, to grant my wish, I shall press no further. Yet perhaps you will favor another. Might you decide my future peace of mind?

LÉONTINE.   My advice, sir, is to wait for Hermocrate; he is the better choice for consultation.

PHOCION.   No. In this instance you are my preference. I need reasoning that is compassionate. I need a heart whose severity is tempered with indulgence. Such a sweet hybrid flowers among your sex, not mine, so please hear me out; I call upon your prunish, your prudent reservoir of ... goodness.

LÉONTINE.   I know not what prompted your remarks, but your rank begs attention. Do speak. I listen.

PHOCION.   Several days ago, while traveling in these parts, I espied a lady on her constitutional. She did not see me. *(Sigh.)* Shall I paint her portrait for you? Her size is majestic — without being large. Never have I seen such a divine countenance — why it is the only face in the world where one could witness the most tender charms wedded to the most imposingly modest and austere air. How could one not fall in love with her — however fearfully? She is young, but not in youth's first folly — that age disappoints me. No, she is of that truly lovable age, that age that dare not name its number, that age when one enjoys all that one is, no more, no less — the age at which the soul, undissipated, adds a dazzling ray of finesse to beauty.

LÉONTINE.   I don't know of whom you speak. Such a woman as you describe is not in my acquaintance unless your portrait has been retouched.

PHOCION.   The likeness resting in my heart is a thousand times greater than that which I have painted for you, my lady. I was just passing through, but the sight of this wondrous *sylph* transfixed me. She was speaking to someone. From time to time she smiled, and I perceived in her gestures, which belied her grave and modest bearing, an ineffable sweetness and generosity.

LÉONTINE.   *(Aside.)* Who on earth is he describing?

PHOCION.   She withdrew. When I inquired after her, I learned she was the sister of a famous, respected man.

LÉONTINE.   *(Aside.)* What is happening to me?

PHOCION.   She is completely unmarried, living in retreat with him. Like all sublimely virtuous souls, she prefers innocent repose to the wicked tumult of the world. Upon learning this, my reason followed my heart's example and gave itself to her forever.

LÉONTINE.   *(Moved.)* I can listen to you no further. I don't know what love is. I could not advise you on a matter I do not understand.

PHOCION.   Pray, let me finish, and may the word love not offend you. If I love, if I worship her lovable countenance, it is because my soul is in sympathy with all the beauties of her soul.

LÉONTINE.   Let me take leave of you. I am expected within.

PHOCION.   I am done, Madame. Filled as I am with such heartfelt emotion, I swear to love her all of my life. *(Carefully.)* Which means I promise to consecrate all my days in service of Virtue. I must talk to her brother and obtain his permission to stay. And then I plan to use submissive love, industrious respect, and tender homage to prove my boundless passion for her.

LÉONTINE.   *(Aside.)* How do I escape such a snare?

PHOCION.   I wished to present myself to her brother. Instead I found her and tried vainly to win her support. She slammed the gates on my heart. And now, in my wretched state, I only have recourse to you, my lady. I throw myself at your feet. O, pity me! *(Phocion falls to her knees.)*

LÉONTINE.   What are you doing?

PHOCION.   I beseech your advice and help with her.

LÉONTINE.   After what I've just heard, I'll have to ask the gods.

PHOCION.   The counsel of the gods rests in your heart. Trust their noble instructions.

LÉONTINE.   In my heart? O heavens, you want me to consult the enemy of tranquillity?

PHOCION.   How could a noble action upset your tranquillity?

LÉONTINE.   Phocion, you claim to revere virtue. Is coming

17

to surprise it reverent?

PHOCION.   Is adoring it surprising it? *(Pause.)*

LÉONTINE.   What are your intentions?

PHOCION.   I consecrate my life to you. Don't block my passage. Grant me several days in your midst — that is my sole desire. If you agree to this, Hermocrate will.

LÉONTINE.   Keep you here? You, who love me?

PHOCION.   What is wrong with a love that only increases my respect?

LÉONTINE.   Can a virtuous heart demand that which it is not? Do you want me to lose my heart? What did you come here for, Phocion? What you propose is inconceivable to my being! What an adventure! Must my reason perish in flames? I who have never loved — must I love you? The time is late for me to become sensitive. You are young and attractive; I am neither one nor the other.

PHOCION.   What a strange response.

LÉONTINE.   I admit that a small share of beauty befell me, and Nature imparted some of her charms upon my person. But I have always scorned these things. Perhaps you make me regret that. *(Pause.)* I am ashamed. I have them no more, or the little that remains will soon fade.

PHOCION.   You cannot convince my eyes that what they see is not there.

LÉONTINE.   I am no longer what I was.

PHOCION.   All true souls share the same birthdate. *(Pause.)* You know what I ask; you know I shall press Hermocrate on this point. If you don't favor my wishes, I'll simply — and in great pain, mind you — *DIE!*

LÉONTINE.   I don't know what to do. Hermocrate is coming. I will help you. *(Hermocrate enters with Agis and Harlequin.)*

HERMOCRATE.   Is this the young man in question?

HARLEQUIN.   I saw him first. And I made sure to give him all your best wishes in advance.

LÉONTINE.   *(Rapidly, as if one breath.)* Hermocrate, you see before you the son of illustrious Phocion whose esteem for *you* brings him hither. He loves wisdom, travels for instruction; several of your peers have had the pleasure of taking

18

him in; he desires the same welcome from us; he begs with an eagerness that merits approval; I promised to do my utmost in his favor; I do so, and doing so, I leave you now. *(Léontine rushes off.)*

AGIS.   If my desire is worthy of consideration, I concur with Léontine, good lord, and leave. *(Agis rushes off.)*

HARLEQUIN.   As for me, my voice will out shout them both. *(He remains.)*

HERMOCRATE.   *(Examining Phocion.)* What do I see?

PHOCION.   I bless their noble intercessions on my behalf. Good Lord, please recognize my deep respect for you. *(Phocion bows.)*

HERMOCRATE.   I thank you, sir, for all honor you do me. As for recognition, permit me to say that a disciple such as you does not appear to need a master such as I. Nevertheless, I would like to question you. *(To Harlequin.)* Privately. You. Go. *(Harlequin exits.)* Either I am mistaken or you are not unknown to me. Sir.

PHOCION.   Me? Sir?

HERMOCRATE.   I have some suspicions which crave enlightenment.

PHOCION.   What are these suspicions?

HERMOCRATE.   First, you are not called Phocion.

PHOCION.   I'm not?

HERMOCRATE.   The man whose name you assume is currently in Athens, or so a letter from Mermicide informs me.

PHOCION.   Phocion is a common name.

HERMOCRATE.   An alias is the least of your falsehoods.

PHOCION.   *(Aside.)* He remembers the forest.

HERMOCRATE.   Second, that attire does not suit you. Admit it. I've seen you somewhere before, my lady.

PHOCION.   *(Feigning surprise.)* You speak the truth, sir.

HERMOCRATE.   Yes. You blushed in front of me.

PHOCION.   If I blush, I do so unjustly. I disavow such an action. My disguise cloaks no nefarious design.

HERMOCRATE.   I see behind the deception, and there is nothing praiseworthy about it. It does nothing but discredit your sex. The idea to come here and steal my pupil Agis, to lure him into danger, to throw his heart into deadly disorder — this plan, it seems to me, ought to give you plenty to blush about, young lady.

PHOCION.   Who? Agis? You mean that boy just now? That is your suspicion? How could you of all men make this outrageous accusation? *You?* The gods, who truly know my heart, should have spared me this abuse. No, my lord, I did not come here to upset Agis's heart. Your hands may have raised him; your lessons may have fortified him, but I wouldn't need a disguise to conquer his childish heart. If I loved *him*, why I'd only have to look at him to woo and win. *(Pause.)* I look elsewhere, I seek someone more difficult to surprise. My eyes are powerless before this man, my charms are impotent — I cannot count on them as a resource — they would not please. So I hide them in manly raiment.

HERMOCRATE.   If you're not thinking of Agis, what is the connection between your infatuation and your proposed sojourn here?

PHOCION.   Agis! Agis! Always Agis! Do not mention him again. I repeat, I think not on him. Do you need incontestable proof of that? My sex is not too proud to offer it. My pride is nobler than yours — you wait and see. But if it is still a question of suspicions ... the one I love, shall he give me his hand? Here is mine. *(Pause.)* Agis isn't here to accept my offer.

HERMOCRATE.   To whom is it addressed?

PHOCION.   Naming Hermocrate is but gilding the lily.

HERMOCRATE.   Me?

PHOCION.   You have been duly instructed.

HERMOCRATE.   *(Disconcerted.)* So I have. Me, the object of someone's heart?

PHOCION.   Listen to me. Allow me to justify my oath.

HERMOCRATE.   All justification is useless. Fear not my philosophy, but am I made to be loved? You attack a solitary and untamed soul. Love is a stranger to me. My severity needs must rebuff your youth and charm. My heart can do nothing for yours.

PHOCION.   I don't ask it to share my feelings. I have no

20

hope for that. But let me finish. I told you that I loved you — no, let me speak.

HERMOCRATE. My eminent reason forbids me from hearing more of this.

PHOCION. But my glory and my honor — which I just compromised by the way — force me to continue. I only aspire to appear worthy to you. There is nothing dangerous about me — except my now-humiliated charms, and the weakness of my sex, which you scorn.

HERMOCRATE. Your sex I prefer to ignore altogether.

PHOCION. Yes, my lord, I love you, but do not deceive yourself. This is no common penchant. I tell you that I love you, because I need confusion in order to say it, because confusion will perhaps cure me, because I need to blush out my weakness to conquer it. I don't say I love you to make you love me back. I do it so you can teach me not to love you anymore. Hate love, scorn love — I gladly consent — just teach me to be like you. Teach me to banish you from my heart. Forbid the attraction I feel for you. I don't demand your love — I *crave* it. Kill my craving!!!

HERMOCRATE. My lady, here is my prescription. I do not want to love you, period. *(Pause.)* May my indifference cure you; may it end a discourse poisonous to all who hear it.

PHOCION. Indifference! I might have known you'd reduce me to indifference! Is that how you respond to my courage in exposing my feelings to you? The wise man, the famous sage, the celebrated scholar, is he a kingdom unto himself?

HERMOCRATE. I am not ... that ... my lady.

PHOCION. So be it! But grant me time enough to discover your faults. Let me finish! Men speak of you everywhere. Your reknown is widespread.

HERMOCRATE. Now it is I who blush.

PHOCION. Excuse the heart that delights in praising its love. *(Pause.)* My name is Aspasie, and I have lived, like you, in solitude. I was mistress of my fate, ignorant of Love, scornful of all men who tried to kindle it in me.

HERMOCRATE. Listening degrades me.

PHOCION. I was in my customary state when I first met

you, when we were both walking. I did not know who you were at first; my thoughts were private. Yet, one look at you and I was moved — my heart cried out Hermocrate. Hermocrate.

HERMOCRATE.   In the name of the virtue you say you cherish, Aspasie, please come to a point. I can bear no more of this story.

PHOCION.   The tale seems frivolous to you — but believe me, the need to recover my reason is not.

HERMOCRATE.   The need to recover mine is even greater. As blunt as I am, I still have eyes, you still have charms, and you say you love me.

PHOCION.   I? Charms? My lord, do you spy them? Or are you afraid to feel them?

HERMOCRATE.   I cannot expose myself.

PHOCION.   If you avoid me, it follows that you fear them. You don't love me yet, but you fear loving me. More than enough for now. Hermocrate, you will love me.

HERMOCRATE.   My answers are coming out wrong.

PHOCION.   Oh my lord, let's go find Lady Léontine. I wish, as you know, to reside here awhile. *(Dimas enters as Phocion starts to exit.)* You can tell me later what you have decided about my stay.

HERMOCRATE.   Proceed Aspasie, I'll follow. *(She is gone.)* I got lost in that conversation. Come here Dimas — you see that young man ahead of me? I charge you to observe him carefully — follow him as closely as you can — check to see whether he seeks out Agis, understand? You know I admire your zeal — the best way for you to prove your worth is to follow my instructions. Exactly.

DIMAS.   Said and done, milord. I'll report any news. Later if not sooner. *(Hermocrate exits.)* Maybe never.

END ACT ONE

ACT TWO

Dimas and Harlequin appear on opposite sides of the stage.

DIMAS.   Hey!

HARLEQUIN.   Ho!

DIMAS.   Listen. I tell you since these new people showed up, there's no talking to you. You're always whispering off to the side with that squire's valet.

HARLEQUIN.   That's my good breeding, my friend. I love you no less even if I have dropped you.

DIMAS.   Oh, so it's genteel to dishonor your old friend. Friendship's like wine: the older the better.

HARLEQUIN.   A tasteful comparison; we'll drink to that whenever you want — on me.

DIMAS.   Big spender. Shake the money tree, eh? You've come into some.

HARLEQUIN.   Never you mind.

DIMAS.   Squeakin' squirrel.

HARLEQUIN.   I do not merit such abuse.

DIMAS.   I know the guests been greasing your palm. I've got eyes — I saw you counting your share.

HARLEQUIN.   *(Aside.)* He's right. Now he's counting on a share for himself.

DIMAS.   *(Aside.)* Now I've nabbed him. *(Aloud.)* Listen up, friend. Master's got some rumpus in his reason.

HARLEQUIN.   Did he see me count my share?

DIMAS.   Worse, much worse! He has put my eyes on the whole affair. He's having me play fox to sniff out the thoughts of our two fine strangers on the sly, tail their intentions, you hear?

HARLEQUIN.   And ... friend fox?

DIMAS.   I only tell my master.

HARLEQUIN.   Pretty please.

DIMAS.   First off, I have to tell him what these people really are.

HARLEQUIN.   Watch what you're saying.

DIMAS. What's it to you? I keep no secrets from him.

HARLEQUIN. You know who they are then?

DIMAS. The plant and the root, my friend, the plant and the root.

HARLEQUIN. I thought I was the only one who knew —

DIMAS. You? You know nothing!

HARLEQUIN. Yes I do!

DIMAS. You can't — they're too tricky for you.

HARLEQUIN. Don't flatter yourself. They told me so themselves.

DIMAS. Told you what?

HARLEQUIN. That they're women.

DIMAS. They're what?

HARLEQUIN. Women. *(Pause.)* You didn't know?

DIMAS. I do now.

HARLEQUIN. Seed sower! Ill-mannered raker! Hedgehog —

DIMAS. Women? This is choice.

HARLEQUIN. I am such an ass.

DIMAS. Here's a tale with profit in it. This is prime. Here's the stuff of blackmail.

HARLEQUIN. You mean you'd cut my throat, Dimas?

DIMAS. What do I care? That's choice — women pulling stumps behind the gardener's back, and *I* found them. I'll prune 'em all.

HARLEQUIN. You've got a sweet tooth for money.

DIMAS. Damned if I don't. Whose money might that be, friend?

HARLEQUIN. I'll have my lady finance you and buy back my blunder. I promise.

DIMAS. I warn you; small farmers don't come cheap. Tell me, how much did you get off the lady? Small change?

HARLEQUIN. She gave me twenty pieces of gold.

DIMAS. Twenty gold pieces? She's a regular charitable institution! So why'd she come take cover?

HARLEQUIN. Agis took her heart for a walk.

DIMAS. Sweet of him.

HARLEQUIN. She disguised herself to ransack his.

DIMAS. Sweet of her. Well, it all spells booty to me. And

24

that little Hermidas — is she —

HARLEQUIN.   That's a heart *I'm* set to plunder.

DIMAS.   She's not spoiling for you. Here they come. Have their species trot forward. *(Phocion and Hermidas enter.)*

HERMIDAS.   *(To Phocion, referring to Harlequin.)* I can't talk to him now. He's with the gardener.

DIMAS.   *(To Harlequin.)* They won't come near me. Tell them I've been made abreast of their personages.

HARLEQUIN.   *(To Phocion.)* Fear not, good mistress, but I've been a chatterbox.

PHOCION.   Good mistress? To whom do you refer, Harlequin?

DIMAS.   Cut your corn, lady. I outfoxed him.

PHOCION.   Quoi? Vous m'avez trahi? O justes cieux! Il faut me venger! Misérable! Scélérat! Lâche! Traître!

HARLEQUIN.   I left no stone unturned.

DIMAS.   I know your heart's bent, Ma'am, and I know what you're set to do to Agis's.

PHOCION.   Corine, my project has failed.

HERMIDAS.   Don't be discouraged, my lady. Every general needs foot soldiers. We need only buy off the gardener too — am I right, Dimas?

DIMAS.   Missy, I share your opinion completely.

HERMIDAS.   Name your price.

DIMAS.   You get what you pay for.

HARLEQUIN.   He isn't worth a ducat.

PHOCION.   *(Giving him some money.)* Is this advance enough to tide you over, Dimas? If you keep quiet, you shall thank the heavens above — *forever* — for your association in this adventure.

DIMAS.   Silence is golden.

HARLEQUIN.   And if I'd held my tongue, all that money would have landed in my pocket. My wages are buying off that green-thumbed vulture.

PHOCION.   Rejoice that I'll enrich the both of you. Earlier Hermocrate seemed disposed that I could stay here, but I fear he's changed his mind — right now he's trying my case with his sister and Agis, who both want me to stay. Tell me the truth now: did you let anything slip out about Agis in front of him? Conceal nothing from me.

HARLEQUIN. Upon my word, o great and beautiful mistress, the answer is no. This false friend here is the only one who dragged anything out of me.

HERMIDAS. Prudence should have cut your tongue in two.

PHOCION. If you said nothing, then I fear nothing. Corine will tell you how far I've succeeded. Now that Dimas is on our side, divide the work between them, Corine. It's a matter of wooing the dispositions of brother and sister. Here comes Agis — go quickly! And make sure Hermocrate doesn't find us together. *(They exit and Agis enters.)*

AGIS. Dear Phocion, I've been looking for you. I am worried that Hermocrate is not so disposed to grant your wish. I've never felt so annoyed with him. His allegations are unreasonable, of all things. But Léontine also spoke most favorably of you. So don't be discouraged, dear Phocion. I beseech you as your friend, keep pressing your suit. We can convince him.

PHOCION. You "beseech" me, Agis? Does this mean you find my presence here ... not unpleasant?

AGIS. If you leave, I can expect only ennui.

PHOCION. Only you can keep me here.

AGIS. Then your heart shares my feelings?

PHOCION. A thousand times more than I can say.

AGIS. Pray, may I ask you for proof of that? This is the first time in my life that I've savored the taste of friendship. You reap the first fruits of my heart. *(Pause.)* Do not teach me the pain of severed friendship: stay.

PHOCION. Me teach you that, Agis? How could I do that without also falling victim to it?

AGIS. How your response touches me! Listen. Do you remember you told me that it was up to me to see you always? Here is what I have imagined.

PHOCION. Tell me.

AGIS. I don't know how I can leave this house. Important reasons — you will know them someday — keep me here. But you Phocion, you who are master of your destiny, wait for me here to decide my own. Promise me to stay nearby.

You'll be alone, true, but we'll be together. Can the world offer anything sweeter than the intercourse of two virtuous, loving hearts?

PHOCION.   I promise you, Agis, wherever you are, that is what I'll call the world.

AGIS.   I'm so happy. The gods made sure I was born in calamity. Your promise, I feel, is the first of many favors they have in store for me.

PHOCION.   I do have one worry. *Love* might soon intercede and alter our tender feelings. The pull of a friend holds nothing against the push of a mistress.

AGIS.   Love, Phocion? You have yet to know me well. May the sky render your heart as love-proof as mine. My upbringing, my sentiments, my reason have all closed my heart to love. Why, when I stop to think of it, I hate the odious sex that goads men to love!

PHOCION.   *(Seriously.)* That sex is an object of hate, Agis?

AGIS.   I shall flee it all my life.

PHOCION.   Sir, that oath alters everything between us. I promised you I would remain, but that is now no longer possible. Honor forbids me. And so I take my leave. I do not wish to fool you. The friendship you have pledged to me forbids such base knavery.

AGIS.   Knavery? What are you talking about? Why this change? What did I say that could possibly upset you so?

PHOCION.   True friends never lie to one another. I cannot lie to you. You spoke a moment ago of the pain of severed friendship. Soon I shall feel it.

AGIS.   Sever our friendship?

PHOCION.   You are still my friend, but I am no longer yours. *(Pause.)* I am but one of those objects hateful to you. Yes, a hateful object I!

AGIS.   What?

PHOCION.   My lord, my garb dupes you. It shelters an unlucky girl who escaped the persecution of Princess Léonide. My name is Aspasie. I am the last in an illustrious family. My inheritance has forced me to flee the land of my birth. The Princess wants to yoke me to one of her relatives. I loathe

the beast in question. After my refusal, I learned that she was going to have me kidnapped. My only recourse against such violence was to run away in this disguise. I had heard of Hermocrate and his learned solitude. So I came here, seeking retreat — incognito. I met you; you offered me amity; I saw you were worthy of mine. I confide in you even as I speak — that is proof of my feeling. And despite your principled hate which now must overrule your friendship, I will never withdraw mine.

AGIS.   I don't know what to think.

PHOCION.   Then let me collect your thoughts for you. Adieu.

AGIS.   No!

PHOCION.   Hermocrate wishes me to go. You suffer my feminine presence painfully. My departure should satisfy you both. I'll go and seek gentlemen whose goodness *will* grant asylum to an unfortunate girl. *(She begins to leave.)*

AGIS.   No, my lady, stop ... it's true your sex is dangerous — but the unfortunate are always respectable.

PHOCION.   You hate me, sir. *(She begins to leave.)*

AGIS.   No, no, Aspasie. I must be sensitive to your piteous condition. If it's necessary, I'll force Hermocrate toward consenting to your stay. Your unhappiness commands me.

PHOCION.   So you'll only be acting out of pity, I suppose. Oh this has been a discouraging adventure. The young lord they picked out for me is looking better all the time. Maybe I should just run myself in to him.

AGIS.   My lady, I don't advise it. The hand must follow the heart. So I've always heard tell. They say the unhappiest fate of all is a union with someone you don't love. Life becomes then an unbearable fabric of listless tissue. Virtue, in such cases, even as it defends us, crushes the soul. But maybe you feel you would willingly love the beast chosen for you.

PHOCION.   No, my flight is proof of that!

AGIS.   Take care then, that some secret fondness doesn't lead you to another man.

PHOCION.   That cannot happen. I resemble you on this point. My heart has never been moved until now — when it felt such friendship for you. And if you don't retract your feeling, my heart need never feel anything else.

AGIS.   *(Confused.)* Don't ever go near that evil princess again! *(Pause.)* I still feel as I did.

PHOCION.   You still like me then?

AGIS.   And forever, my lady. Even more now ... since there's nothing to fear. Since we feel so ... friendly, right: right? So like ... that's all we ... no doubt ... and ....

PHOCION and AGIS.   *(Sighing.)* Ahhhh!

PHOCION.   My lord, as a friend you are overwhelmingly worthy. *(Dreamy.)* As a lover, you are only too qualified. *(Catching herself.)* I say that as a friend.

AGIS.   I hope never to become a lover.

PHOCION.   *(Crushed.)* No? *(Catching herself.)* Let's set love aside. It's dangerous even to speak of it.

AGIS.   Right ... uh ... your servant Hermidas is looking for you. Hermocrate must be free now. Permit me to join him. *(Agis exits. Harlequin and Hermidas enter.)*

HARLEQUIN.   Have no fear, Lady Phocion, your conversation had three guards.

HERMIDAS.   Hermocrate never turned up, but his sister is looking for you. She was asking Dimas where you'd gone to. She looks sad — evidently old stoneface won't budge.

PHOCION.   He resists in vain! I'll sculpt him to my pleasure, or all the art of my sex is worthless.

HARLEQUIN.   And does Lord Agis promise anything? Has his heart simmered enough?

PHOCION.   Two more interviews and he'll be cooked clean through.

HERMIDAS.   Seriously?

PHOCION.   Yes, Corine. The gods have shown me Love's reward.

HARLEQUIN.   *(To Hermidas.)* May they reward me too.

HERMIDAS.   Fresh! Shush, there's Léontine. Let's go.

PHOCION.   Did you give Harlequin his instructions?

HERMIDAS.   Of course, my lady.

HARLEQUIN.   You'll be charmed with my learning. *(They exit. Léontine enters.)*

PHOCION. I was going to hunt for you, Madame. I know what has happened. Hermocrate has refused to give his word.

LÉONTINE. Yes, Phocion. My brother, with what looks to me like groundless ... mulishness, has refused to make a decision. I know you are going to tell me to press harder, but I've come to tell you I'll do nothing of the kind.

PHOCION. Nothing of the kind, my dove?

LÉONTINE. NO! His refusal has called me back to reason.

PHOCION. You deem this a return to reason? This? Léontine, this isn't possible; leaving is a sacrifice my heart cannot make for you. Me leave you? Where shall I find the force to do so? Where have you left me? Look at my situation — I am calling upon your virtue now. I interrogate your virtue — let it be the judge between us. I am here with you; you know that I love you; you see me penetrated by the most tender passion, *you* inspired it, and *I* should leave? Oh, Léontine, ask me for my life, tear my heart to bits — my life, my heart, yours, they're yours yours yours! Don't ask the impossible.

LÉONTINE. *(Aside.)* What ... vivid ... fluctuations! *(Aloud, grandly.)* No Phocion. Never have I felt more the necessitous obligation of your imminent departure.

PHOCION. Translation please?

LÉONTINE. You must go. *(Pause.)* I wash my hands of this affair. O just heavens! Joined to the impetuousness of your heart, what would I become? Is it my obligation to uphold this swarm of passionate expressions that escape your lips? Must I always battle, always resist, and never win? Phocion, you want to inspire me to love, don't you? You don't want me to feel the pain of loving you, but that is what I feel. So go, I beg of you. Leave me in this horrific state.

PHOCION. Save me, Léontine. The thought of leaving you drives me mad. I don't know how to live without you; if I go, it is to fill the pockets of my despair. You see? I don't know what I'm saying anymore.

LÉONTINE. And because *you're* desolate, I have to love you? I like that very much — it's tyranny.

PHOCION. Do you hate me?

LÉONTINE.   I should.

PHOCION.   Then are the dispositions of your heart favorable?

LÉONTINE.   I choose not to listen to them.

PHOCION.   I suppose not. As for me, I cannot keep from following them —

LÉONTINE.   *(Exasperated.)* Oh, shut up. I hear somebody. *(Harlequin enters and silently stands between them for a moment.)*

PHOCION.   What is your servant doing, Madame?

HARLEQUIN.   Since he doesn't know you, sir, Lord Hermocrate has ordered me to examine your conduct.

PHOCION.   But as long as I am with Madame, my conduct needs no chaperone. Tell him to withdraw, Madame.

LÉONTINE.   It is I who should make the withdrawal.

PHOCION.   *(Whispered to Léontine.)* If you go without promising to speak in my favor, I shall no longer speak from reason.

LÉONTINE.   *(Moved.)* Good heavens no!!! *(To Harlequin.)* Hence, Harlequin. Your presence isn't necessary.

HARLEQUIN.   Is too. You don't know who you're dealing with. This gentleman here isn't as wise as a wizened old girl like yourself. No, he wants to tart up your reason.

LÉONTINE.   What do you mean, Harlequin?

HARLEQUIN.   A little while ago, his valet — that sly piece — accosted me and asked: Is there any way we can be friends? Oh, with all my heart, says I — How happy you must be here — Not bad at all — Such honorable masters — Most admirable, says I — Your mistress is so attractive — She's divine — Tell me, has she had any suitors? — As many as she wanted — Has she any now? — As many as she wants — Does she feel like getting married? — What she feels like isn't my affair — Will she remain a maiden? — I can't vouch for that — Who courts her, who doesn't, who comes, does anyone come? And so and so, so I said, by the way is your master in love with her? — Shush, we hope to stay here. But we do have riches and passion enough for ten households and —

PHOCION.   *(Cutting him off.)* Enough!

31

HARLEQUIN. *(To Léontine.)* You see how worried he is now? He'll tell you the rest.

LÉONTINE. Hermidas was only ... having fun with you. Isn't that right, Lord Phocion? *(Phocion doesn't respond.)*

HARLEQUIN. Aha! Aha! Cat got your tongue? Dear mistress, I see your heart is on vacation from your reason. Phocion is giving it the grand tour even as I speak. I'm going to make Hermocrate come to your defense. *(He starts to exit.)*

LÉONTINE. Where are you going? Stop, Harlequin. I don't want him to know I've been made love to!

HARLEQUIN and PHOCION. You've been what?

LÉONTINE. I mean to say — I've been broached by love.

HARLEQUIN and PHOCION. Beg pardon?

LÉONTINE. Love has entered my vocabulary.

HARLEQUIN. *(Pause.)* Well if you've befriended the scamp, there's no need for me to cry "Thief." How easily wisdom accommodates itself. Adieu, madame. Never forget the discretion of your humble servant, who wishes you all the best, then shuts his trap. *(Harlequin exits.)*

PHOCION. Have no fear, my lady. I'll pay for his silence.

LÉONTINE. Blackmail! What next? This is some kind of dream. You see what you've exposed me to! Oh no, here comes somebody else. *(Hermidas enters, carrying a portrait that she gives to Phocion.)*

HERMIDAS. Here's what you asked for, sir. See if you're happy with it. It would be a much finer likeness if the subject had sat for me.

PHOCION. Why did you bring it to me in front of my lady? Let's see — ah yes, it is indeed her face. There is her noble, refined air, and all the fire of her eyes. Although it seems to me that her eyes are still more fiery than that.

LÉONTINE. *(Piqued.)* You speak apparently of a portrait.

HERMIDAS. Give it back, sir, and I'll make her eyes *burn.*

LÉONTINE. Might one see it before it's whisked away?

PHOCION. It is not finished, my lady.

LÉONTINE. Well, if you have your reasons for not revealing it, I won't insist.

PHOCION.   *(Quickly.)* Here it is. You will give it back.

LÉONTINE.   Who is this? It's me. What is this?

HERMIDAS.   It's you.

PHOCION.   I never want to lose sight of you. Your tiniest absence is agony. A moment is a lifetime. This portrait will temper the sickness. Now give it back.

LÉONTINE.   I shouldn't, but so much love on your part stunts my courage.

PHOCION.   *(Softly.)* My love doesn't inspire you the least little bit?

LÉONTINE.   *(Her admission at last.)* Alas! I didn't want it to happen, but perhaps I shall never be the mistress of it. *(She returns the portrait.)*

PHOCION.   Oh, you overwhelm me with joy!

LÉONTINE.   Now that I love you, will my heart stop?

PHOCION.   Don't promise me your heart, Léontine, tell me that I have it.

LÉONTINE.   True, too true for words.

PHOCION.   Then I can stay — and you'll talk to Hermocrate?

LÉONTINE.   I need some time to resolve myself to our union.

HERMIDAS.   Shhh, change the subject — Dimas is coming.

LÉONTINE.   No one must see how my heart has been moved. Goodbye Phocion. Fear not. My brother will consent. *(Léontine exits and Dimas enters.)*

DIMAS.   The philosopher's grazing over this way, all dreamy-like. Give me the field, my lady. I'll clip him to your fancy!

PHOCION.   Courage Dimas! I'll come back when he's gone. *(Phocion exits and Hermocrate enters.)*

HERMOCRATE.   Did you watch Phocion?

DIMAS.   I was going to bring you up to date.

HERMOCRATE.   So. You've discovered something. Is he often with Agis? Does he look for him?

DIMAS.   Oh no. No, way I sees it, he's got another tree to graft.

HERMOCRATE.   What does that mean?

DIMAS.   Means you're a man of merit, a man with large

dimensions.

HERMOCRATE.   What does *that* mean?

DIMAS.   Your wisdom, your virtue, and your face beg praise.

HERMOCRATE.   Oh, and why such enthusiasm from you of all people?

DIMAS.   Me? I tells it like I hears it. And it's all sighing and anguish around here. Alas and alack and all that — how I love him, this man, this agreeable gent.

HERMOCRATE.   I don't know who you're talking about.

DIMAS.   You. And a boy who is a girl.

HERMOCRATE.   No one fits that description here.

DIMAS.   You know Phocion, right? Well, clothes make her man. The rest is pure girl.

HERMOCRATE.   What are you raving about?

DIMAS.   And she's full of attractions. You must be a happy pappy being the target of all those attractions. I heard 'em talking out loud and they said they was waiting for the most mortal man ... no, the most perfect mortal to be found in the whole pack of mortal men — the mortal called Hermocrate.

HERMOCRATE.   Who? Me?

DIMAS.   After you, who? Listen to this.

HERMOCRATE.   Say no more.

DIMAS.   Looking only to obey you, a little while ago while I was chopping in the brush, I was spying on her and her Hermidas — who's a her too — I hopped that hedge all fox-like and came out another end. And I heard 'em gossiping. Phocion said straight off: Ah Corine, this is what's what; no cures for me; I love him too much, this man, I don't know what to do or say — But my lady have your beauty speak for you — Ha, this beauty is no money under the mattress, he still wants me to leave! — Patience my lady — But where does all that wisdom and learning get him?

HERMOCRATE.   Surely you paraphrase.

DIMAS.   Hold on, I'm about done — but what does he say to you when you speak to him, my lady? — He scolds me, and I get all mad. He plays the wise man, I do the same. — I pity you, he says. — But here I am all changed, I say. —

34

But have you no shame, he says. — Where does shame get me, says me. — But your virtue, my lady? — But my torment, my lord? — What — virtues never get married —

HERMOCRATE.   Enough, Dimas. Silence.

DIMAS.   I think you better cure this girl child, master — why don't you fall sick for her too? Make her your wife. If you never pollinate, your family'll be so much dead wood. A crying shame that. Speakin' familiar and family-like now, when you get sick with Phocion, could you put in a good word for me with the chambermaid? I feel my own sickness coming on.

HERMOCRATE.   Why not speak for yourself?

DIMAS.   I know all the tunes master. I just don't know the words.

HERMOCRATE.   Be discreet Dimas. I order you to be discreet. It would be embarrassing for the person in question if her situation were known. As for me, I'll set things straight when I see her. (*Hermocrate exits with a loud groan. Phocion enters.*)

PHOCION.   So what does your master think, Dimas?

DIMAS.   First he seems disposed to keep you.

PHOCION.   So far so good.

DIMAS.   Then on the other hand, he hasn't said that you can stay.

PHOCION.   That doesn't follow.

DIMAS.   He doesn't follow himself. (*Groans.*) That was his parting word on the subject. All that philosophy — he hasn't got an ounce of it left. Out the window and into the mulch.

PHOCION.   A portrait just unbuckled his sister's prudence. I've got one left for him. All according to my original plan. Yet Agis is avoiding me. We haven't spoken since he found out I'm a woman. He talks to Corine, not me!

DIMAS.   He's heading this way, miss. Could you take care to remember my fortune at the end of the story?

PHOCION.   Consider it done.

DIMAS.   Many thanks to ye. (*Dimas exits and Agis enters.*)

AGIS.   Aspasie, why do you flee when I approach?

PHOCION.   Why do you flee when I approach?

AGIS. I am bothered by something.

PHOCION. What?

AGIS. There is a person that I love, well, I am ignorant as to whether I like her as a friend or love her as a — anyway, since I'm still an apprentice on the subject, I've come to ask you for instruction.

PHOCION. I think I know this person.

AGIS. You should have no difficulty. When you came here, you know I loved neither thing nor person.

PHOCION. Yes. And since my arrival, you've met only me.

AGIS. Draw your conclusion.

PHOCION. It is I. *(Pause.)* Or so it follows.

AGIS. *(Softly.)* It does follow. It is you, Aspasie. And so I ask you, "Where am I?"

PHOCION. First, tell me where I am, because I am in the same state for someone I love.

AGIS. For whom, Aspasie?

PHOCION. Whom? The reasons I drew to conclude that you love me — are they not common to both of us?

AGIS. It is true that you had never loved before you arrived.

PHOCION. Yes, and A.) I feel differently now. B.) I've met only you. The rest is clear.

AGIS. So, your heart pines for me, Aspasie.

PHOCION. How long you've been at the solution! Yet all this knowledge doesn't make us any wiser on the subject. We loved each other before we started worrying about it. Now that we do know, do we love each other the same way, or differently?

AGIS. If we were to tell each other what we feel, perhaps that would settle matters.

PHOCION. Let's see then. Was it painful for you to avoid me a little while ago?

AGIS. The pain was infinite.

PHOCION. Hmmm … that's a bad start. Were you avoiding me because your heart was troubled, because it was full of unspeakable feelings?

AGIS. There you have me. A perfect diagnosis.

PHOCION.   Yes. There I have you, but I must warn you that your heart won't get better just because I took its pulse correctly. I still have your eyes to check.

AGIS.   My eyes look at you with a pleasure that goes beyond spectacles! I would give my life for you. I would give a thousand if I had them.

PHOCION.   It's useless to interrogate you further. It's love.

AGIS.   Oh no!

PHOCION.   Damning proof — love in your expression, love in your heart, love in your eyes, love as it should ever be.

AGIS.   Love as it has never been before. *(Pause.)* Now that I've shown you what is in my heart, can I see yours?

PHOCION.   Agis, that's so sweet. Really. *(Pause.)* No. My sex can speak all it wants on the subject of friendship. Of her love, not a word. Besides, you're too tender at this point, and too abashed, I fear, by your tenderness. If I told you my secret now, you might melt away, and where would I be?

AGIS.   You spoke of my eyes. Yours seem to tell me that you are not indifferent to me.

PHOCION.   Well, if my eyes do the talking, I'm beyond reproach. They voice my love for you.

AGIS.   O merciful heavens above! Her sentiments match mine! The charms of her speech have thrown me into passion's chasm!

PHOCION.   But there is more to love than this, Agis. One must have the liberty to say it to oneself, to put oneself in the state of always being able to say it freely, openly. Out loud. And Lord Hermocrate, who governs you ...

AGIS.   I respect and love him. Yet I feel already that a heart should have no governor. I'll have to see him before he speaks to you. He could send you away today, and we need time to plan. *(Dimas appears U. and sings to halt their conversation.)*

PHOCION.   Agis, go to him right away and come right back. I have some other things to tell you.

AGIS.   And I you.

PHOCION.   Go now — if we're seen too long together, I'll be discovered. Adieu.

AGIS.   Lovely Aspasie, I take my leave. I promise you, never will Hermocrate feel so beleaguered. *(Agis exits. Dimas comes D.)*
DIMAS.   *(Rapidly to Phocion as he exits.)* High time lover boy went — here comes the rival! *(Hermocrate enters.)*
PHOCION.   Finally you appear. The ennui and the solitude you left me in will not lessen my affection. Sadder yes, but no less tender am I.
HERMOCRATE.   Other affairs have occupied me, Aspasie. This is no longer a question of affection. Dimas knows who you are. *(No response.)* Need I say more? He overheard the secret of your heart. *(No response.)* Neither one of us can depend on his discretion. Your stay here is henceforth unfeasible — you would be terribly wronged. For your honor's sake, you must leave.
PHOCION.   Leave, sir? You would send me away in such a condition? A thousand times more troubled than I was before I came? What have you done to cure me? Wonderful wise Hermocrate has brought me no virtuous assistance that I can speak of.
HERMOCRATE.   May your affliction heal itself by what I tell you now. You thought me wise; I daresay you loved me for it. I am not wise at all. A true sage would hold himself responsible for your peace of mind. Do you know why I send you away? I am afraid that your secret will explode and damage the esteem that I am held in by others; this means I sacrifice you to my arrogant fear of not appearing virtuous. That way I won't have to worry whether I am or not. This makes me only a vain man for whom true wisdom is less important than the miserable, fraudulent *imitation* he makes of it! There you have me — the object of your love.
PHOCION.   Oh, I've never loved him so much!
HERMOCRATE.   What did you say?
PHOCION.   My lord, is that your only weapon against me? You only increase my ardor and tenderness for you when you expose, with pitiless courage, your desire to cover your own. And you say you aren't wise! You astonish my reason with subtle proof to the contrary!
HERMOCRATE.   Wait, my lady. Did you believe that I was

susceptible to all the ravages love wreaks in other men? The blackest soul, the most vulgar lovers, the maddest knaves and damsels, never feel the agitations that pierce my breast — worries, jealousies, ecstasies have swept through me! Do you recognize Hermocrate in this portrait I paint for you? The universe is full of people who resemble me now! Renounce your love, my lady, a love that any man chosen randomly deserves as much as I.

PHOCION.   No, I repeat, if the gods themselves were susceptible, they would be just like Hermocrate! Never was he more noble, never more worthy of my love, and never my love more worthy of him. You spoke of my honor. I feel honorable to have created even the smallest ecstasy in you. Sir, I seek peace for my heart no more. The oath you made has restored peace in my heart's kingdom. You love me. I am tranquil.

HERMOCRATE.   I have one last word for you then. If you don't leave, then I will reveal your secret. In doing so, I will dishonor myself. I dishonor the man you love, and this affront will reflect back on you.

PHOCION.   Then I go. I go secure in my revenge. And since you love me, may my revenge fester in your heart. Enjoy the fruits, if you like, of your cruel reasoning. I came to ask you for defense against my love; you gave me no help except to vow you loved me in return; and now, *after* your sacred vow is made, you send me away! After a vow that redoubles my tenderness! Oh how the gods will loathe this wisdom preserved at the expense of a young heart cruelly tricked, a confidence cruelly betrayed, and virtuous intentions ridiculed, indeed *victimized*, by your ferocious opinions! *(Phocion bursts into tears.)*

HERMOCRATE.   Please cry in moderation, my lady — someone's coming.

PHOCION.   Oh, first you decimate me, then you will me to silence.

HERMOCRATE.   *(Seriously.)* You have moved me far more than you think — just don't blubber *now. (Harlequin runs in, pursued by Hermidas.)*

HERMIDAS.   Give me that! It's not yours!

HARLEQUIN.   Loyalty forbids me — I must warn my master.

HERMOCRATE.   What's the meaning of all this?

HARLEQUIN.   Foul play, Lord Hermocrate. An affair of consequence that only the devil and these characters here know about.

HERMOCRATE.   Explain yourself.

HARLEQUIN.   I just now discovered this young man here in the position of a scribe! Yes, you heard right, a scribe! He was daydreaming, shaking his head, admiring his work. I noticed alongside him a palette with gray, green, yellow, and white — he was dipping a plume into it. I crept up behind him to look at the original — but what do I find? This was no scribe! No scribe at all! No words, no speeches — he was writing down a *face! (Pause.)* This face, this face ... was you, Lord Hermocrate.

HERMOCRATE.   Me?

HARLEQUIN.   Your own face, except smaller. Why the nose you walk around with is bigger than the entire miniature! Is it fair, I ask you, to shrink people's faces, to diminish the immense sweep and grandeur of their features? Look at yourself. *(He gives Hermocrate the portrait.)*

HERMOCRATE.   Well done Harlequin. I'll discover the meaning of this.

HARLEQUIN.   Just don't forget to have him paint in the other two-thirds of your face. *(Harlequin exits.)*

HERMOCRATE.   Why have you painted me? What were you thinking?

HERMIDAS.   I wanted to have the portrait of an illustrious man.

HERMOCRATE.   You do me too much honor.

HERMIDAS.   And I knew that this portrait would please a certain someone who could not ask for it herself.

HERMOCRATE.   Who is this person?

HERMIDAS.   My lord ...

PHOCION.   Silence, Corine.

HERMOCRATE.   What do I hear? What are you saying, Aspasie?

PHOCION.   No more questions. You make me blush.

HERMOCRATE.   My composure is slipping away.

PHOCION.   I don't know how to bear this last blow.

HERMOCRATE.   And I ... how this ordeal deranges me.

PHOCION.   Corine, how could you let Harlequin surprise you?

HERMOCRATE.   *(His admission.)* You have triumphed, Aspasie, you win, I surrender to you. You may have my portrait. It belongs to you.

PHOCION.   I won't keep it unless your heart abandons it to me.

HERMOCRATE.   Nothing in me shall prevent you from having it.

PHOCION.   Then you must value mine. Here it is. *(She gives him her portrait. He presses it to his lips.)*

HERMOCRATE.   Do you find me humiliated enough? No more quarrels. *(He tries to kiss Phocion.)*

HERMIDAS.   I forgot your ears! Might Lord Hermocrate permit me to finish his likeness? It will only take a moment.

PHOCION.   Do not refuse. We are alone.

HERMOCRATE.   *(Pleading.)* Aspasie, do not expose me to any risks — someone might surprise us.

PHOCION.   You said this is my moment of triumph. Let us savor it. Your eyes look at me with a tenderness and a humility that must be preserved. You never see your looks, my lord. You have no idea how fetching they are. Proceed, Corine.

HERMOCRATE.   Hurry.

HERMIDAS.   Tilt your head a bit, please.

HERMOCRATE.   Oh you have reduced me so.

PHOCION.   Your heart doesn't blush at my reduction.

HERMIDAS.   Raise your chin.

HERMOCRATE.   Must I, Aspasie?

HERMIDAS.   Now turn to the right. *(Pause.)* Turn.

HERMOCRATE.   Please stop. Agis is coming. You may go, Hermidas. *(Hermidas exits. Agis enters.)*

AGIS.   I've come to plead with you my lord. Allow Phocion to stay. Please.

41

HERMOCRATE. *(Worried.)* You wish him to stay, Agis?

AGIS. Nothing on earth would please me more. I swear to you I would be very angry if you made him leave.

HERMOCRATE. I had no idea that you were already so taken with one another.

PHOCION. *(Very formally.)* Indeed. Our conversations have been most infrequent.

AGIS. *(Hurt.)* I hope I haven't interrupted your conversation. Perhaps that is why you treat me so coldly.

PHOCION. Agis!

AGIS. Pardon me.

PHOCION. Wait! *(Agis exits.)*

HERMOCRATE. Now why is Agis so forward? In all these years I've never seen him so interested in anything as much as you. *(Pause.)* How well do you know him? Have you revealed yourself to him? Do you abuse my feelings?

PHOCION. I'm so happy I could burst with joy! You've just told me you're jealous.

HERMOCRATE. No.

PHOCION. In so many words, yes. You've made me so happy — my heart thanks you for such injustice. Hermocrate is jealous. He cherishes me, he adores me. So what if he insults me! He may be unjust, but he loves me! *(Pause.)* Agis is not far off; I still see him — have him come back, call him sir. I'll go look for him myself — I'll speak to him, and you'll see whether I merit your lovely suspicions.

HERMOCRATE. No, Aspasie. I see my mistake. Your frankness is reassuring. Don't call him. Forgive me. No one must know that I love you yet. Give me time to think.

PHOCION. I consent and I forgive. Here comes your sister. I'll leave you two alone. *(Aside.)* Dear gods, pardon my scheme. How I pity his weakness. *(Phocion exits and Léontine enters.)*

LÉONTINE. There you are. I've been asking after you everywhere. No one can sit still today.

HERMOCRATE. What do you want, Léontine?

LÉONTINE. Where do you stand with Phocion? Do you still plan to send him away? He holds *you* in such high esteem, speaks so well of *you,* that I promised him that he could stay. I gave him my word, brother. And don't try to change my mind. I never retract a statement.

HERMOCRATE.   I could never change your mind, Léontine. Since you made a promise, he will stay as long as *you* like, sister.

LÉONTINE.   *(A pause.)* How obliging you've become. It shocks me, brother. In truth, Phocion deserves the favor.

HERMOCRATE.   I have measured his full worth.

LÉONTINE.   And besides, it will be so nice for Agis to have a playmate, don't you think? No one should be alone at that age.

HERMOCRATE.   *(With a little sigh.)* That or any other age.

LÉONTINE.   You're right. One has moments of sadness. Even I get bored now and then. Or very often. Or all the time.

HERMOCRATE.   Who doesn't get bored? Is not man born for society?

LÉONTINE.   Did we know what we were doing when we forsook mankind and came to this retreat? It was such a rapid decision. Such a painful decision to make so ... rapidly.

HERMOCRATE.   Go on, sister. I haven't your courage.

LÉONTINE.   After all, mistakes can be remedied. Man can, fortunately, change his mind.

HERMOCRATE.   And change for the better.

LÉONTINE.   *(Tentatively.)* A man at your age would be welcome everywhere if he wanted to change his station.

HERMOCRATE.   And you, who are younger and more attractive than I ... permit me to say I am not anxious for *you.*

LÉONTINE.   Oh brother, few young men are your equal ... permit me to say the gift of your heart would not go unopened.

HERMOCRATE.   As for yours ... men would fall in line to gain your heart and give you theirs.

LÉONTINE.   *(Shyly.)* Would you be surprised if I said I have some prospects?

HERMOCRATE.   I'd be more surprised if you had not.

LÉONTINE.   And you?

HERMOCRATE. *(With a smile.)* Who knows? My lips are sealed.

LÉONTINE. How wonderful for you, brother. *(Pause.)* Hermocrate. The gods invented marriage. The gods are married. We have no more wisdom than the gods ...

HERMOCRATE. *(Softly.)* Ergo ...

LÉONTINE. Ergo ... I believe a husband is as worthy as a hermit. Think. Adieu. *(Léontine exits.)*

HERMOCRATE. I see the both of us are in a rare and tender state. I wonder who she has set her sights upon. Maybe someone as young for her as ... Aspasie is ... for me. Oh how weak man is. *(Long pause.)* If this be man's destiny, I suppose we must submit.

END ACT TWO

ACT THREE

Hermidas and Phocion are discovered in the garden.

PHOCION.   Come talk to me, Corine. Infallible success is mine. Would you have believed I'd conquer both philosophers? Hermocrate and Léontine fell one after the other. Now they both want to marry me secretly. I can't begin to tell you how many measures they've already taken for their imaginary nuptials. Why, it's impossible to chart where Love has led their wise heads. They're off the map. *(Sighs.)* Agis. We need to talk. I think I've blown it with him. He loves me as Aspasie. Could he hate me as Princess Léonide?
HERMIDAS.   No my lady. Finish him off. After all that Léonide has done and will do for him, he'll find her more lovable than plain Aspasie.
PHOCION.   I daresay I agree with you. But his family perished because of mine.
HERMIDAS.   Your father inherited the throne — he didn't usurp it.
PHOCION.   I love him. I fear him. But I must act certain of success. Have you had my letters sent to the estate?
HERMIDAS.   I sent them with the messenger Dimas gave me. You'll soon have news. You addressed them to Ariston. What are his orders?
PHOCION.   I bade him to follow the messenger with guards and a coach. Agis will leave this garden a prince. Post yourself at the gate, Corine, and come get me the moment Ariston arrives. Go put the crowning touch on all that you have done for me.
HERMIDAS.   You're not through with Léontine yet — here she comes-a-courting. *(Hermidas exits and Léontine enters.)*
LÉONTINE.   Dearest Phocion, one thought: the die is cast.
PHOCION.   Yes, may the heavens be praised.
LÉONTINE.   *(Dramatically.)* I shall depend on no one but myself and my love. We shall be united for all eternity. You

45

sent for the coach, didn't you? I told you I didn't want to create a spectacle near the house, but I fear the measures we've taken don't appear entirely decent. Instead of leaving together, wouldn't it be better if I went ahead first and waited for you in the city?

PHOCION.   Leave by yourself? How cunning of you, my pet.

LÉONTINE.   Love emboldens me. Two hours hence — I shall be hence. But Phocion, you will fly to my side?

PHOCION.   The sooner you leave, the sooner I'll fly.

LÉONTINE.   You can't give me anything but love.

PHOCION.   Yours is priceless.

LÉONTINE.   No other man in the world could make me take this step.

PHOCION.   An innocent little step, really, and you run no risk if you run now!

LÉONTINE.   I love your enthusiasm — may it last forever!

PHOCION.   And may you always be eager in return — because right now your turtle steps try my patience.

LÉONTINE.   I must confess to you that a sadness ineffable, fleeting takes hold of me at times.

PHOCION.   I only feel joy.

LÉONTINE.   There's my brother. He cannot find me in emotional undress. *(Léontine exits.)*

PHOCION.   Again with the brother! There's really no end to these two! *(Hermocrate enters.)* I thought you'd be busy arranging our departure.

HERMOCRATE.   Oh my charming Aspasie, if you only knew how divided I feel!

PHOCION.   Oh if you only knew how weary I feel dividing you! Again and again. One can never be too sure with you.

HERMOCRATE.   Forgive my agitation. My heart promises to be more decisive in the future.

PHOCION.   Ah! Your heart takes so many attitudes, Hermocrate, you can be as agitated as you like, just hurry, unless you want the wedding to take place here.

HERMOCRATE.   *(Sighs.)* Ahhhh …

PHOCION.   Sighs expedite nothing.

HERMOCRATE.   I have one last thing to tell you, something that pains me very much.

PHOCION.   One more last thing more? You never conclude, do you?

HERMOCRATE.   I shall entrust everything to you. I sacrificed my heart, and soon I shall be yours. Then there will be no more secrets between us.

PHOCION.   Except?

HERMOCRATE.   I've raised Agis ever since he was a boy. I cannot abandon him so quickly. Do you think he might live with us for a while? We can send for him after the honeymoon. He can be our common interest.

PHOCION.   Who is he?

HERMOCRATE.   You've heard tell of Cléomenes. Agis is his son. He escaped from prison in his infancy.

PHOCION.   Your confidence is in safe hands.

HERMOCRATE.   I've sheltered him so carefully over the years. What would he become in the hands of a princess who breathes his death?

PHOCION.   Come now. She is reputed to be fair and generous.

HERMOCRATE.   Her blood is neither one nor the other.

PHOCION.   They say she would marry Agis — if only she knew him. They are the same age after all.

HERMOCRATE.   Whatever she wants is beside the point. The righteous hate Agis bears against her would prevent such a union.

PHOCION.   I would have believed that the glory of pardoning one's enemy might equal the honor of hating her forever. Especially when the enemy is innocent.

HERMOCRATE.   No, the throne is too high a price for this pardon. Friends are fomenting a war against her. Agis will enlist.

PHOCION.   Will no one defer to the Princess? Submit to her rule? Or will they just kill her?

HERMOCRATE.   Since hers is only an inherited guilt, they need not kill her, just imprison her.

PHOCION.   I think that's all you better confess for now,

47

dear. Finish packing.

HERMOCRATE.   Adieu, dear Aspasie. I've only another hour or two to spend here. *(Hermocrate exits.)*

PHOCION.   Agis must be waiting for an opportunity to speak to me. This hate he bears for me makes me tremble. *(Dimas and Harlequin enter.)* More counselors? Will I never be rid of them? And what do you want?

HARLEQUIN.   Your servant, my lady.

DIMAS.   I salute you, my lady.

PHOCION.   Not so loudly, please.

DIMAS.   Never fear, we're alone.

PHOCION.   What do you want?

HARLEQUIN.   A trifle.

DIMAS.   I'm here to square your debts.

HARLEQUIN.   To see how much we're worth together.

PHOCION.   Out with it. I'm pressed for time.

DIMAS.   Have I done good work?

PHOCION.   You've both served me well.

DIMAS.   And your plan is working?

PHOCION.   I have one last thing to reveal to Agis, who, as you speak, is waiting for me.

HARLEQUIN.   Very good. If he's waiting, we won't press.

DIMAS.   It's a black, marvelous affair we've sold.

HARLEQUIN.   There are no comparable rascals in the kingdom.

DIMAS.   I threw your heart all over the neighborhood.

HARLEQUIN.   Portraits to trap faces —

PHOCION.   Get to the point.

DIMAS.   Your scheme is soon to bloom. How much will you yield for the harvest?

PHOCION.   What do you mean?

HARLEQUIN.   Buy the rest of the adventure. Our price is reasonable.

DIMAS.   Give us your business, or I'll squeal.

PHOCION.   Didn't I promise to make your fortune?

DIMAS.   Give us your word in gold.

HARLEQUIN.   After all —

HARLEQUIN and DIMAS.   Henchmen are forgotten once

the dirty work is done.

PHOCION.   What insolence!

DIMAS.   Could be, could be.

PHOCION.   You anger me with this impertinence. Here is my answer. Should you foil my plan, should you commit an indiscretion, you'll atone for it in a prison cell. You don't know who I am. But I warn you I have the power to lock you both away. If, on the other hand, you remain silent, I shall keep every promise I made you. Choose. As for the present, I order you to leave. Right your wrong with swift obeisance.

DIMAS.   *(To Harlequin.)* Well, do we keep up the sass?

HARLEQUIN.   No, that's the garden path to jail. I prefer anything to four stone walls. *(They exit.)*

PHOCION.   I did well to upbraid them. *(Agis enters.)* Agis. At last.

AGIS.   We meet again, Aspasie. At last I can speak to you in perfect liberty. I almost hate Hermocrate and Léontine for all the hospitality they've shown you; you're never alone. But you are so lovable, who would not love you? How sweet it is to love you, Aspasie.

PHOCION.   What pleasure to hear you say that, Agis. Tell me, this tenderness, this charming candor, is it proof of everything? Nothing could rob me of it?

AGIS.   No — the only way would be to cease breathing.

PHOCION.   I've something to tell you. You don't know me.

AGIS.   I know your charms; I know the sweetness of your soul; nothing could tear me from them. They're enough for me to adore my whole life long.

PHOCION.   O Gods! The more I cherish love, the more I fear losing it. I've kept my birth from you, Agis.

AGIS.   You don't know who I am either — nor can you know the terror I feel to unite my life with yours. O cruel Princess, I have so many reasons to despise you!

PHOCION.   Who are you talking to — about, Agis? Which princess do you hate so much?

AGIS.   I shrink from pronouncing her name. She who reigns, Aspasie. My enemy and yours. Princess Léonide who

49

— someone's coming.

PHOCION.   Hermocrate, the eternal interrupter. I'll come back as soon as he leaves. Our destiny hangs on a word. You hate me — without knowing it.

AGIS.   Me, Aspasie?

PHOCION.   No more for now. Break with Hermocrate. *(Phocion exits.)*

AGIS.   *(Alone.)* I don't understand what she means. I can't leave Hermocrate without telling him my plans. *(Hermocrate enters.)*

HERMOCRATE.   *(Troubled.)* What I have to say to you, my prince, I don't know where to begin.

AGIS.   What is wrong?

HERMOCRATE.   Something that you could never have imagined, something I'm ashamed to confess to you, but something, after much reflection, I feel I must tell you.

AGIS.   That's quite a preamble. *(Pause.)* What has happened to you?

HERMOCRATE.   I find I am as weak as any other man.

AGIS.   My lord, to what type of weakness do you refer?

HERMOCRATE.   The most common weakness of all, the most excusable for everyone else — but the most unexpected for me. *(Pause.)* You know what I've thought of the passion called love.

AGIS.   Yes, and to speak frankly, you've exaggerated a bit on that topic.

HERMOCRATE.   If you like, but what could you expect? A solitary man who meditates, who studies, who kept commerce with his mind, never his heart. A man shrouded in an austerity of his own design can hardly be expected to bear judgement on certain things. He would go too far.

AGIS.   You fell into excess.

HERMOCRATE.   What didn't I say against love? To me this passion was crazy, extravagant, unworthy of a reasoning soul; I called it delirium when I didn't know what I was talking about. I consulted neither nature nor reason. I was criticizing the very heavens.

AGIS.   Yes, because in the end, man is born to love.

HERMOCRATE.　Exactly. Everything revolves around that feeling.

AGIS.　A feeling that might one day avenge itself upon you and your scorn for it.

HERMOCRATE.　Too late.

AGIS.　What?

HERMOCRATE.　I have been duly punished.

AGIS.　Seriously?

HERMOCRATE.　Prepare yourself for a change in character. If you love me, come with me. I'm getting married.

AGIS.　This is the source of your confusion.

HERMOCRATE.　Oh Agis, it is very painful to switch philosophies.

AGIS.　I congratulate you for it. The only gap in your knowledge was the purpose of man's heart.

HERMOCRATE.　I have received quite a lesson of late, I assure you. Passion's industry has truly come to call. And just in time I feel to ... I was seen several times in the forest — someone developed an attraction for me — the person tried to cease and desist, but could not. Lest her true sex risk unwelcome, she disguised herself, became the most handsome of men. She came here, and I instantly recognized the deception. I wanted her to go; I even thought *you* were the object of her attention — she swore this was false. She said: "I love you. My hand, my fortune belong to you, along with my heart. Give me yours in return or cure mine — yield to my affections or teach me to conquer them; teach me indifference or share my love." This was said to me with such eyes, in such dulcet tones, they would have conquered the most ferocious and obstinate of philosophers.

AGIS.　Sir, this tender lover disguised, have I seen him here? She came here?

HERMOCRATE.　She is still here.

AGIS.　I only see Phocion.

HERMOCRATE.　He is she. And not a word to Léontine. *(Léontine enters.)*

AGIS.　*(Aside.)* Treacherous woman! What has she gained by deceiving me?

LÉONTINE. *(As nonchalant as she can muster.)* I've come to tell you of a short stay I intend to make in town.

HERMOCRATE. With whom shall you be staying, Léontine?

LÉONTINE. Tatiana — I have news from her — she entreats me to visit.

HERMOCRATE. Then, as I am leaving within the hour, we shall both be gone.

LÉONTINE. You're leaving, my brother? Where shall you be?

HERMOCRATE. With Criton.

LÉONTINE. Really? In town like me! How peculiar that we both have things to do in town. I am recalling our previous conversation. Does your trip carry any mystery on board?

HERMOCRATE. That is a question that makes me ... question the motive of *your* trip. Surely you remember your words, my dear?

LÉONTINE. Hermocrate, let's speak with open hearts. We've found each other out. I'm not going to Tatiana's.

HERMOCRATE. Since you adopt a frank tone, I too shall come clean, I'm not going to Criton's.

LÉONTINE. My heart is taking me on a trip.

HERMOCRATE. Mine has packed my bags.

LÉONTINE and HERMOCRATE. I'm getting married!

LÉONTINE. How astonishing. *(Pause.)* Now that it's out in the open, I believe my beloved and I can get married right here and save travel expenses.

HERMOCRATE. You're right. My heart's delight is here too. We needn't leave either.

LÉONTINE. We can have a double wedding! *(Pause.)* I, for one, don't know who your heart's delight is. *(Pause.)* I'm marrying Phocion.

HERMOCRATE. Phocion!

LÉONTINE. Yes, Phocion!

HERMOCRATE. You me — the man who sought us out, the man whose cause you championed?

LÉONTINE. The very one.

HERMOCRATE. Hold on — I'm marrying him too. I — he — we — me! We can't both marry him.

LÉONTINE.   Him? You marry a him?

HERMOCRATE.   Nothing could be truer.

LÉONTINE.   You and Phocion? Is this a new philosophy? Phocion loves me with an infinite tenderness; he had my portrait copied unbeknownst to me.

HERMOCRATE.   Your portrait! It's mine, not yours, that he had copied without my knowledge.

LÉONTINE.   You are mistaken. Here is his portrait — don't you recognize him?

HERMOCRATE.   Here sister, here is its double; yours is a man; mine is a woman. That makes all the difference.

LÉONTINE.   O misery!

AGIS.   Enough! *I'm* marrying her, and I didn't get a portrait!

HERMOCRATE.   You too?

AGIS.   Me three!

LÉONTINE.   I am beside myself with indignation!!!

HERMOCRATE.   This is no time for indignation, Léontine. This impostor has to explain himself — herself! *(Léontine and Hermocrate exit.)*

AGIS.   This is despair. *(Phocion enters.)*

PHOCION.   Agis, look at me. What's wrong?

AGIS.   What have you really come to do here? Which member of our unhappy trio gets to marry you? Hermocrate, Léontine, or Agis?

PHOCION.   I am discovered.

AGIS.   Don't I at least get a portrait? Everybody else did.

PHOCION.   The others would never have received my portrait if I hadn't wanted to give you the person.

AGIS.   I yield you to Hermocrate. Goodbye perfidious one. Goodbye cruel ... cruel ... person! I don't know what to call you. What does one call someone like you? I never met anyone like you. This shall kill me.

PHOCION.   Stop, dear Agis — listen to me.

AGIS.   Let me go, I say.

PHOCION.   No, I'll never let you go. And if you don't pay attention, you'll be the most ungrateful of men.

AGIS.   *I* will? I — whom you deceive?

PHOCION.   I tricked everyone else for you! There was no other way — my snares are proof of my tenderness. You insult the tenderest heart imaginable. You cannot know all the love that you owe me; all the love I bear for you, you cannot know. You will love me, you will hold me in esteem, and you will crave pardon.

AGIS.   I don't understand.

PHOCION.   To gain your heart I did everything I could to abuse those who stood in my way. You were the sole object of my machinations.

AGIS.   How can I believe you, Aspasie?

PHOCION.   Dimas and Harlequin, who know my secret, will second this pledge. Interrogate them. My love is not ashamed to seek the confirmation of servants.

AGIS.   How can what you're saying be possible, Aspasie? Then no one has ever loved as much as you.

PHOCION.   That is not all. This Princess, whom you call your enemy and mine —

AGIS.   She will never spare the son of Cléomenes. If you truly love me, she will make you cry over my death one day.

PHOCION.   I am in a position to make you judge of *her* fate.

AGIS.   I would only ask her to let us arrange our fate together.

PHOCION.   Arrange her life yourself then. You have already delivered her heart.

AGIS.   Her heart? Princess Léonide — is you?

PHOCION.   The full extent of my love is yours entirely. *(Agis falls to his knees.)*

AGIS.   My heart cannot answer you with words. *(Hermocrate and Léontine enter.)*

HERMOCRATE.   What do I see? Agis on bended knee? *(He shows a portrait to Phocion.)* This is a portrait of —

PHOCION.   Me.

LÉONTINE.   *(Showing portrait.)* And this one, varlet, is —

PHOCION.   Me. Shall I withdraw them and return yours?

HERMOCRATE.   This is no time for pleasantries. Who are you? *(Hermidas, Harlequin, and Dimas enter.)*

PHOCION.   I shall tell you. But first let me speak to Corine.

DIMAS.   Master, I warn you, there's a garden full of pike-staffers and ruffian soldiers and fancy carriages.

HERMIDAS.   Ariston has arrived.

PHOCION.   *(To Agis.)* My lord and master, come receive the homage of your subjects. Your royal guard awaits you. It is time to leave. *(To Léontine and Hermocrate.)* You, Hermocrate, and you, Léontine, who first refused to let me stay, learn now the motive of my artifice. I wished to surrender the throne to Agis, and I wanted to be his. Had I used my true identity, I would have rebuffed his heart. I disguised myself to catch it. For this plan to bear fruit, I had to abuse your hearts by turns. There is no cause for complaint. Hermocrate, I leave your heart to the care of your eminent reason. As for yours, Léontine, the revelation of my sex must have already doused the embers of the feelings inspired by my hoax.

END OF PLAY

THE TRIUMPH OF LOVE

Pronunciation Guide

LÉONIDE	Lay - o - NEED
LÉONTINE	LAY - on - teen
HERMIDAS	HAIR - mee - dahss
DIMAS	Dee - MAHSS
HERMOCRATE	Her - MAH - cruh - tee
AGIS	Ah - JHEES
PHOCION	FO - see - awn
CORINE	Kor - EEN
CLÉOMENES	Clay - AHM - uh - neez
LÉONIDES	Lay - ON - uh - deez
EUPHROSINE	You - FRAHZ - uh - nee

PROPERTY LIST

Sundial with moveable dial
Rhinestone tiara (PHOCION)
Black riding crop (PHOCION)
Gold coin (PHOCION)
Velvet money bags (PHOCION)
Louis Vuitton duffle bag (stuffed) (HERMIDAS)
Louis Vuitton shoulder bag (stuffed) (HERMIDAS)
Loose change (not seen) (HERMIDAS)
Pitchfork (DIMAS)
10" clay pot holding small "shrub" (LÉONTINE)
Natural twig basket with handle (LÉONTINE) with:
    leaf samples glued to 6"x4" white cards
    pair of white cotton gardening gloves
    gardening clippers
Camp stool with brocade seat (LÉONTINE)
Garden hose (DIMAS)
Gold-framed portrait of "Léontine" (miniature)
    (HERMIDAS)
Gold-framed portrait of "Phocion as boy" (miniature)
    (PHOCION)
Silver hand mirror (HARLEQUIN)
Gold-framed portrait of "Hermocrate" (HARLEQUIN)
Gold-framed portrait of "Phocion as girl" (PHOCION)
Paint palette with dabs of yellow/green/gray/white paint
    (dry) (HERMIDAS)
Single red rose (LÉONTINE)
Black walking stick with silver knob (HARLEQUIN)
Color paper confetti (DIMAS)
2 books (AGIS)
Hoe (DIMAS)
2 suitcases (LÉONTINE)
Gold ornate music stand
Wood chair with cane seat
White plumed quill
Harp

NEW PLAYS

★ **MOTHERHOOD OUT LOUD by Leslie Ayvazian, Brooke Berman, David Cale, Jessica Goldberg, Beth Henley, Lameece Issaq, Claire LaZebnik, Lisa Loomer, Michele Lowe, Marco Pennette, Theresa Rebeck, Luanne Rice, Annie Weisman and Cheryl L. West, conceived by Susan R. Rose and Joan Stein.** When entrusting the subject of motherhood to such a dazzling collection of celebrated American writers, what results is a joyous, moving, hilarious, and altogether thrilling theatrical event. "Never fails to strike both the funny bone and the heart." –*BackStage.* "Packed with wisdom, laughter, and plenty of wry surprises." –*TheaterMania.* [1M, 3W] ISBN: 978-0-8222-2589-8

★ **COCK by Mike Bartlett.** When John takes a break from his boyfriend, he accidentally meets the girl of his dreams. Filled with guilt and indecision, he decides there is only one way to straighten this out. "[A] brilliant and blackly hilarious feat of provocation." –*Independent.* "A smart, prickly and rewarding view of sexual and emotional confusion." –*Evening Standard.* [3M, 1W] ISBN: 978-0-8222-2766-3

★ **F. Scott Fitzgerald's THE GREAT GATSBY adapted for the stage by Simon Levy.** Jay Gatsby, a self-made millionaire, passionately pursues the elusive Daisy Buchanan. Nick Carraway, a young newcomer to Long Island, is drawn into their world of obsession, greed and danger. "Levy's combination of narration, dialogue and action delivers most of what is best in the novel." –*Seattle Post-Intelligencer.* "A beautifully crafted interpretation of the 1925 novel which defined the Jazz Age." –*London Free Press.* [5M, 4W] ISBN: 978-0-8222-2727-4

★ **LONELY, I'M NOT by Paul Weitz.** At an age when most people are discovering what they want to do with their lives, Porter has been married and divorced, earned seven figures as a corporate "ninja," and had a nervous breakdown. It's been four years since he's had a job or a date, and he's decided to give life another shot. "Critic's pick!" –*NY Times.* "An enjoyable ride." –*NY Daily News.* [3M, 3W] ISBN: 978-0-8222-2734-2

★ **ASUNCION by Jesse Eisenberg.** Edgar and Vinny are not racist. In fact, Edgar maintains a blog condemning American imperialism, and Vinny is three-quarters into a Ph.D. in Black Studies. When Asuncion becomes their new roommate, the boys have a perfect opportunity to demonstrate how open-minded they truly are. "Mr. Eisenberg writes lively dialogue that strikes plenty of comic sparks." –*NY Times.* "An almost ridiculously enjoyable portrait of slacker trauma among would-be intellectuals." –*Newsday.* [2M, 2W] ISBN: 978-0-8222-2630-7

DRAMATISTS PLAY SERVICE, INC.
440 Park Avenue South, New York, NY 10016 212-683-8960 Fax 212-213-1539
postmaster@dramatists.com www.dramatists.com

NEW PLAYS

★ THE PICTURE OF DORIAN GRAY by Roberto Aguirre-Sacasa, based on the novel by Oscar Wilde. Preternaturally handsome Dorian Gray has his portrait painted by his college classmate Basil Hallwood. When their mutual friend Henry Wotton offers to include it in a show, Dorian makes a fateful wish—that his portrait should grow old instead of him—and strikes an unspeakable bargain with the devil. [5M, 2W] ISBN: 978-0-8222-2590-4

★ THE LYONS by Nicky Silver. As Ben Lyons lies dying, it becomes clear that he and his wife have been at war for many years, and his impending demise has brought no relief. When they're joined by their children all efforts at a sentimental goodbye to the dying patriarch are soon abandoned. "Hilariously frank, clear-sighted, compassionate and forgiving." –NY Times. "Mordant, dark and rich." –Associated Press. [3M, 3W] ISBN: 978-0-8222-2659-8

★ STANDING ON CEREMONY by Mo Gaffney, Jordan Harrison, Moisés Kaufman, Neil LaBute, Wendy MacLeod, José Rivera, Paul Rudnick, and Doug Wright, conceived by Brian Shnipper. Witty, warm and occasionally wacky, these plays are vows to the blessings of equality, the universal challenges of relationships and the often hilarious power of love. "CEREMONY puts a human face on a hot-button issue and delivers laughter and tears rather than propaganda." –BackStage. [3M, 3W] ISBN: 978-0-8222-2654-3

★ ONE ARM by Moisés Kaufman, based on the short story and screenplay by Tennessee Williams. Ollie joins the Navy and becomes the lightweight boxing champion of the Pacific Fleet. Soon after, he loses his arm in a car accident, and he turns to hustling to survive. "[A] fast, fierce, brutally beautiful stage adaptation." –NY Magazine. "A fascinatingly lurid, provocative and fatalistic piece of theater." –Variety. [7M, 1W] ISBN: 978-0-8222-2564-5

★ AN ILIAD by Lisa Peterson and Denis O'Hare. A modern-day retelling of Homer's classic. Poetry and humor, the ancient tale of the Trojan War and the modern world collide in this captivating theatrical experience. "Shocking, glorious, primal and deeply satisfying." –Time Out NY. "Explosive, altogether breathtaking." –Chicago Sun-Times. [1M] ISBN: 978-0-8222-2687-1

★ THE COLUMNIST by David Auburn. At the height of the Cold War, Joe Alsop is the nation's most influential journalist, beloved, feared and courted by the Washington world. But as the '60s dawn and America undergoes dizzying change, the intense political dramas Joe is embroiled in become deeply personal as well. "Intensely satisfying." –Bloomberg News. [5M, 2W] ISBN: 978-0-8222-2699-4

DRAMATISTS PLAY SERVICE, INC.
440 Park Avenue South, New York, NY 10016 212-683-8960 Fax 212-213-1539
postmaster@dramatists.com www.dramatists.com

NEW PLAYS

★ **BENGAL TIGER AT THE BAGHDAD ZOO by Rajiv Joseph.** The lives of two American Marines and an Iraqi translator are forever changed by an encounter with a quick-witted tiger who haunts the streets of war-torn Baghdad. "[A] boldly imagined, harrowing and surprisingly funny drama." –*NY Times.* "Tragic yet darkly comic and highly imaginative." –*CurtainUp.* [5M, 2W] ISBN: 978-0-8222-2565-2

★ **THE PITMEN PAINTERS by Lee Hall, inspired by a book by William Feaver.** Based on the triumphant true story, a group of British miners discover a new way to express themselves and unexpectedly become art-world sensations. "Excitingly ambiguous, in-the-moment theater." –*NY Times.* "Heartfelt, moving and deeply politicized." –*Chicago Tribune.* [5M, 2W] ISBN: 978-0-8222-2507-2

★ **RELATIVELY SPEAKING by Ethan Coen, Elaine May and Woody Allen.** In TALKING CURE, Ethan Coen uncovers the sort of insanity that can only come from family. Elaine May explores the hilarity of passing in GEORGE IS DEAD. In HONEYMOON MOTEL, Woody Allen invites you to the sort of wedding day you won't forget. "Firecracker funny." –*NY Times.* "A rollicking good time." –*New Yorker.* [8M, 7W] ISBN: 978-0-8222-2394-8

★ **SONS OF THE PROPHET by Stephen Karam.** If to live is to suffer, then Joseph Douaihy is more alive than most. With unexplained chronic pain and the fate of his reeling family on his shoulders, Joseph's health, sanity, and insurance premium are on the line. "Explosively funny." –*NY Times.* "At once deep, deft and beautifully made." –*New Yorker.* [5M, 3W] ISBN: 978-0-8222-2597-3

★ **THE MOUNTAINTOP by Katori Hall.** A gripping reimagination of events the night before the assassination of the civil rights leader Dr. Martin Luther King, Jr. "An ominous electricity crackles through the opening moments." –*NY Times.* "[A] thrilling, wild, provocative flight of magical realism." –*Associated Press.* "Crackles with theatricality and a humanity more moving than sainthood." –*NY Newsday.* [1M, 1W] ISBN: 978-0-8222-2603-1

★ **ALL NEW PEOPLE by Zach Braff.** Charlie is 35, heartbroken, and just wants some time away from the rest of the world. Long Beach Island seems to be the perfect escape until his solitude is interrupted by a motley parade of misfits who show up and change his plans. "Consistently and sometimes sensationally funny." –*NY Times.* "A morbidly funny play about the trendy new existential condition of being young, adorable, and miserable." –*Variety.* [2M, 2W] ISBN: 978-0-8222-2562-1

DRAMATISTS PLAY SERVICE, INC.
440 Park Avenue South, New York, NY 10016 212-683-8960 Fax 212-213-1539
postmaster@dramatists.com www.dramatists.com

NEW PLAYS

★ **CLYBOURNE PARK by Bruce Norris.** WINNER OF THE 2011 PULITZER PRIZE AND 2012 TONY AWARD. Act One takes place in 1959 as community leaders try to stop the sale of a home to a black family. Act Two is set in the same house in the present day as the now predominantly African-American neighborhood battles to hold its ground. "Vital, sharp-witted and ferociously smart." –*NY Times.* "A theatrical treasure…Indisputably, uproariously funny." –*Entertainment Weekly.* [4M, 3W] ISBN: 978-0-8222-2697-0

★ **WATER BY THE SPOONFUL by Quiara Alegría Hudes.** WINNER OF THE 2012 PULITZER PRIZE. A Puerto Rican veteran is surrounded by the North Philadelphia demons he tried to escape in the service. "This is a very funny, warm, and yes uplifting play." –*Hartford Courant.* "The play is a combination poem, prayer and app on how to cope in an age of uncertainty, speed and chaos." –*Variety.* [4M, 3W] ISBN: 978-0-8222-2716-8

★ **RED by John Logan.** WINNER OF THE 2010 TONY AWARD. Mark Rothko has just landed the biggest commission in the history of modern art. But when his young assistant, Ken, gains the confidence to challenge him, Rothko faces the agonizing possibility that his crowning achievement could also become his undoing. "Intense and exciting." –*NY Times.* "Smart, eloquent entertainment." –*New Yorker.* [2M] ISBN: 978-0-8222-2483-9

★ **VENUS IN FUR by David Ives.** Thomas, a beleaguered playwright/director, is desperate to find an actress to play Vanda, the female lead in his adaptation of the classic sadomasochistic tale *Venus in Fur.* "Ninety minutes of good, kinky fun." –*NY Times.* "A fast-paced journey into one man's entrapment by a clever, vengeful female." –*Associated Press.* [1M, 1W] ISBN: 978-0-8222-2603-1

★ **OTHER DESERT CITIES by Jon Robin Baitz.** Brooke returns home to Palm Springs after a six-year absence and announces that she is about to publish a memoir dredging up a pivotal and tragic event in the family's history—a wound they don't want reopened. "Leaves you feeling both moved and gratifyingly sated." –*NY Times.* "A genuine pleasure." –*NY Post.* [2M, 3W] ISBN: 978-0-8222-2605-5

★ **TRIBES by Nina Raine.** Billy was born deaf into a hearing family and adapts brilliantly to his family's unconventional ways, but it's not until he meets Sylvia, a young woman on the brink of deafness, that he finally understands what it means to be understood. "A smart, lively play." –*NY Times.* "[A] bright and boldly provocative drama." –*Associated Press.* [3M, 2W] ISBN: 978-0-8222-2751-9

DRAMATISTS PLAY SERVICE, INC.
440 Park Avenue South, New York, NY 10016 212-683-8960 Fax 212-213-1539
postmaster@dramatists.com www.dramatists.com